# WHEN WORLDS COLLIDE

iUniverse books may be ordered through booksellers or by contacting:

iUniverse
1663 Liberty Drive
Bloomington, IN 47403
www.iuniverse.com
1-800-Authors (1-800-288-4677)

ISBN: 978-1-4502-6479-2 (pbk)
ISBN: 978-1-4502-6480-8 (ebk)

Printed in the United States of America

iUniverse rev. date: 12/23/10

# WHEN WORLDS COLLIDE

## JAMES G DAVIES

iUniverse, Inc.
Bloomington

OUR COUPLE

WOULD LIKE TO
DEDICATE THIS
'SLICE OF LIFE'
TO;_____
DATED;_____

# "WARNING!"

Do not! - I repeat! - Not!
Not photocopy any part of this book!

Violators will not only be tracked down to be made fun of in any future publishing's, but also quite openly whenever possible jokingly laughed at!

Any sketching or even the remotest similarities in this book to actual persons alive or dead are not only greatly - I repeat 'greatly' unintentional - but truly and honestly outright accidentally coincidental!

The opinions expressed herein are solely those of our two retirees - and do not warrant or intend to incriminate or mock any person or persons within similar situations.

Since it's a proven fact that humor is indeed at times the best of medicines for what may ail you - read on - and on - and only then decide if you really want to pick sides in an ever ongoing confrontation of wits, or is it 'nitwits', as our couple engage in an everlasting battle of humor in the remainder of their happy time together here on this earth.

4

5

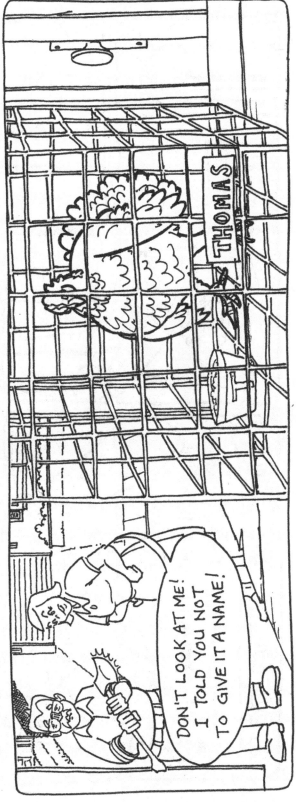

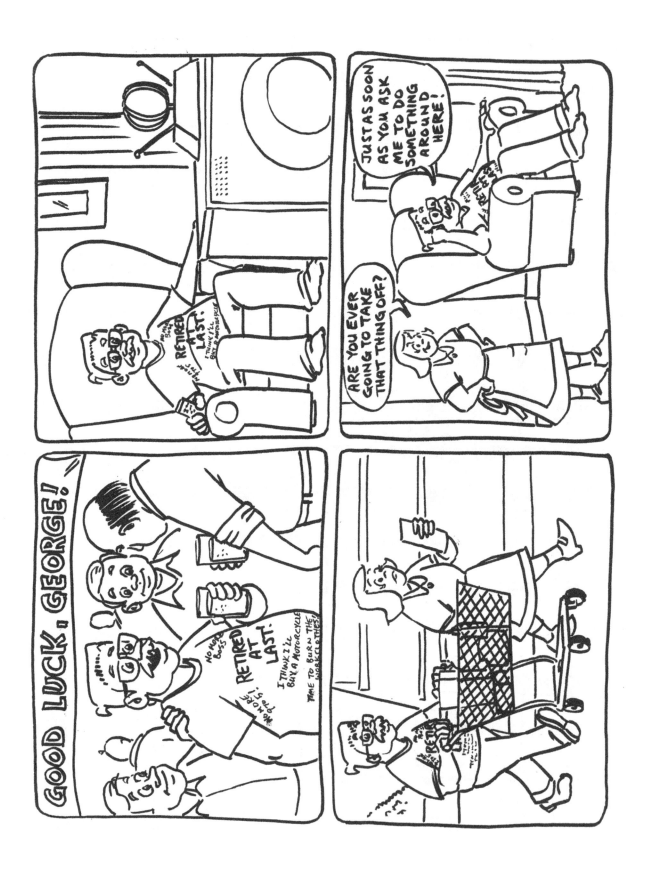

"WOW, HON! THIS ENERGIZED SUPER DUPER T.V. REMOTE THE MEN AT WORK BOUGHT ME AS MY RETIREMENT GIFT, SURE DOES WORK!... COME HERE AND SEE!"

"I TOLD HER, I WAS RETIRED! ... SHE SAYS, I'M NOT! ... I TOLD HER, I WAS RETIRED! ..."

" NOW THAT WE HAVE ALL THIS SPARE TIME ... LET'S RETURN YOUR MOTHER'S VISITS!"

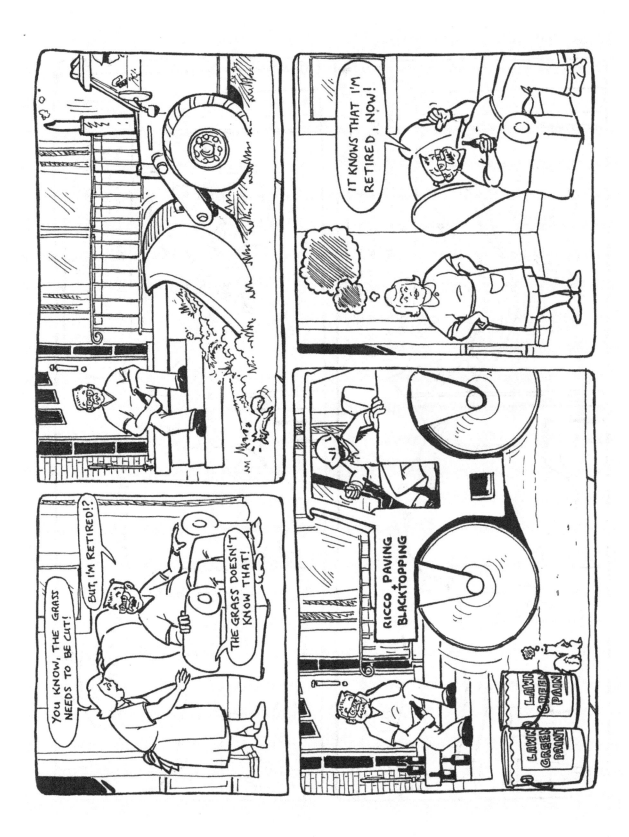

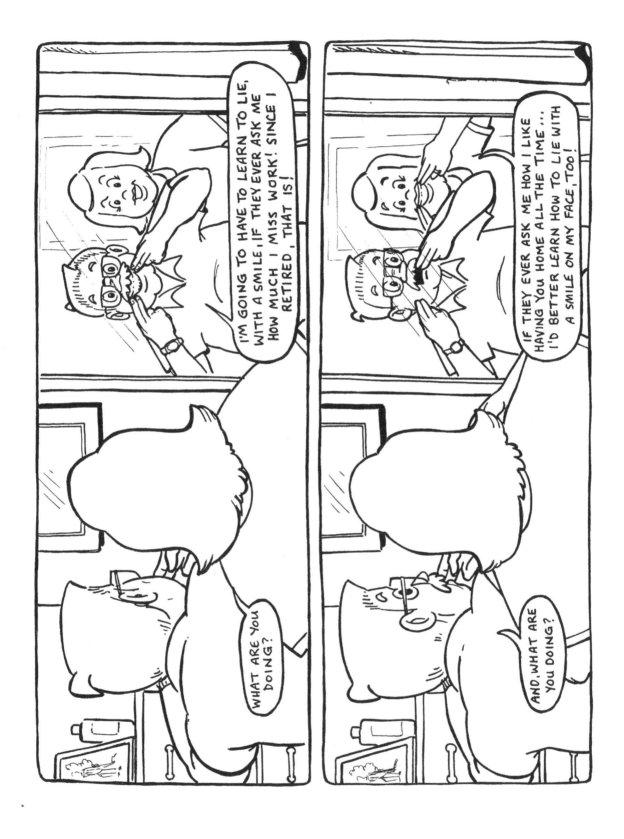

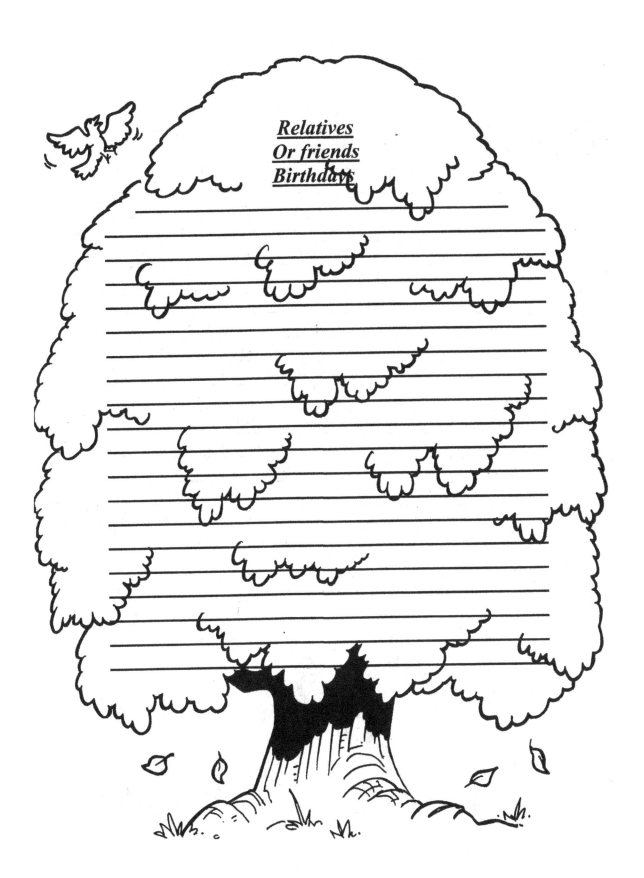

Relatives
Or friends
Birthdays

19

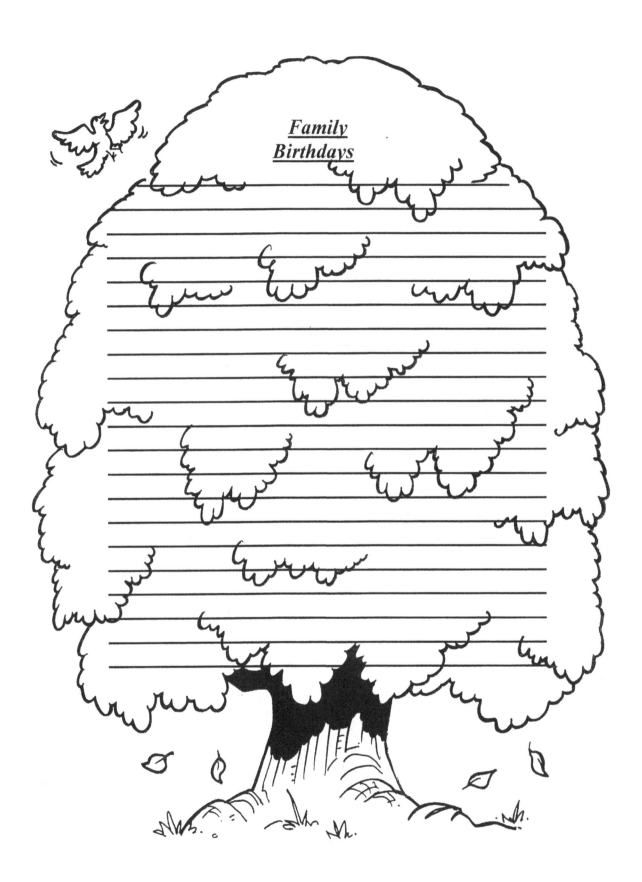

Family
Birthdays

"I ALWAYS SAID THAT WHEN I RETIRED I WAS GOING TO STAY UP AS LONG AS I COULD. WITH MY LUCK, I WON'T BE ANYWHERE NEAR A BED WHEN SLEEP ATTACKS."

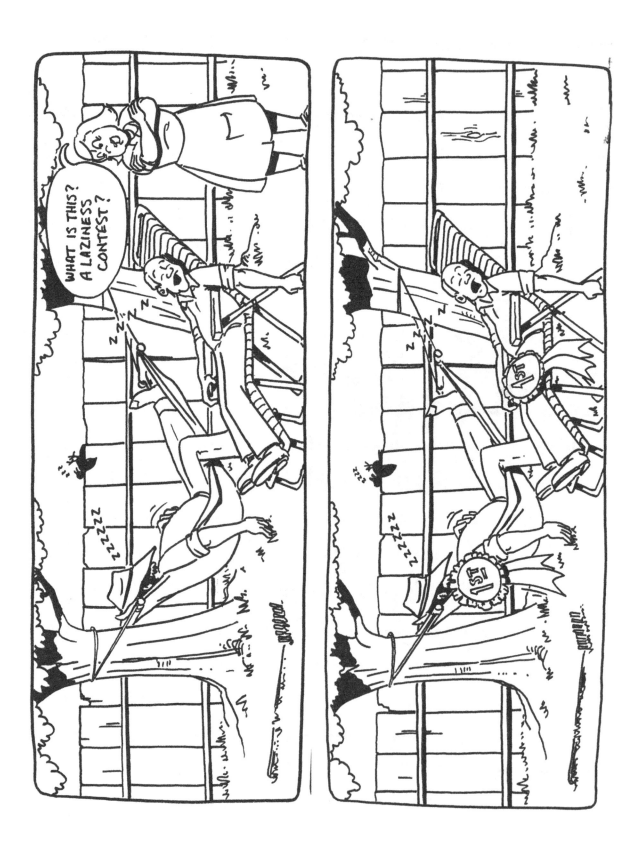

29

36

W
O
R
K
I
T

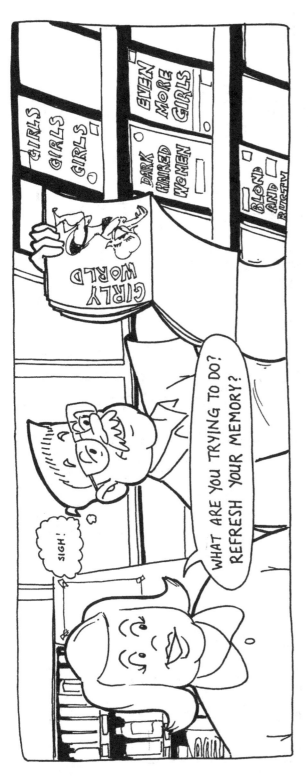

"APPARENTLY, I MISUNDERSTOOD YOU AS TO WHAT TYPE OF HOUSE WE SHOULD OPEN, ONCE WE'VE RETIRED!!"

44

46

**R**

**E**

**C**

**I**

**P**

**E**

48

58

"MY WIFE CAN TALK THE WALLPAPER OFF A WALL! SO! I'VE BEEN THINKING OF GETTING MY EARS PIERCED! NOT MY EARLOBES ... MY EARDRUMS!!!"

## DOCTOR APPOINTMENTS

69

71

73

82

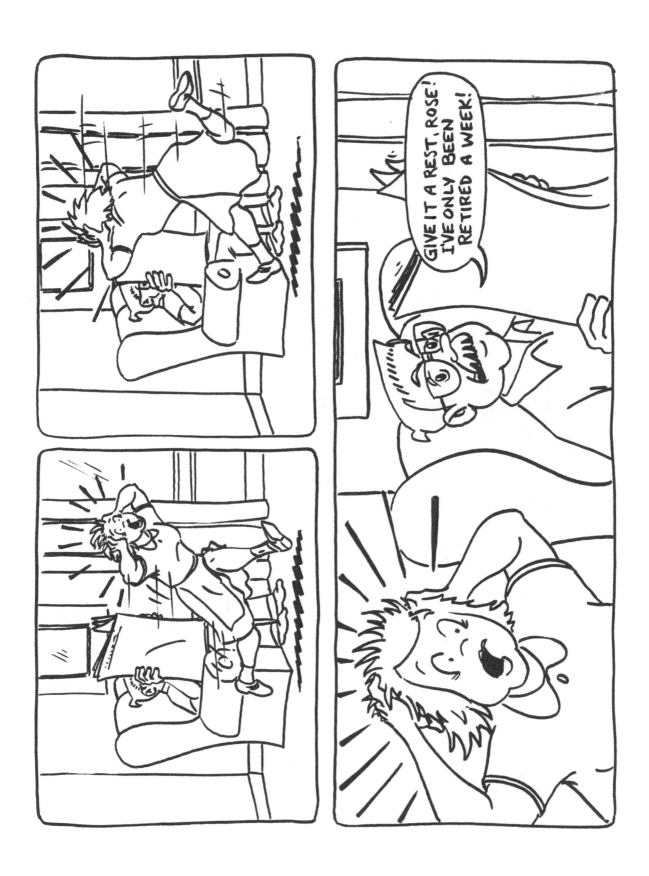

91

92

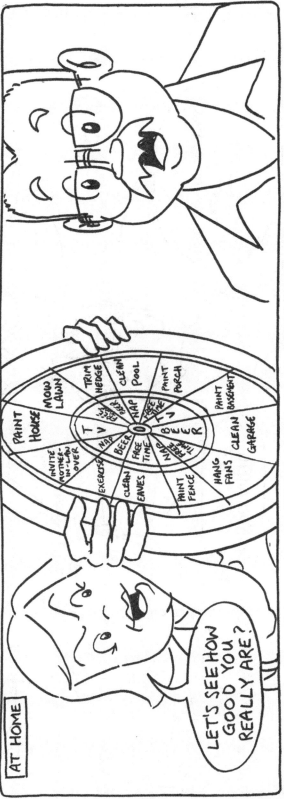

97

98

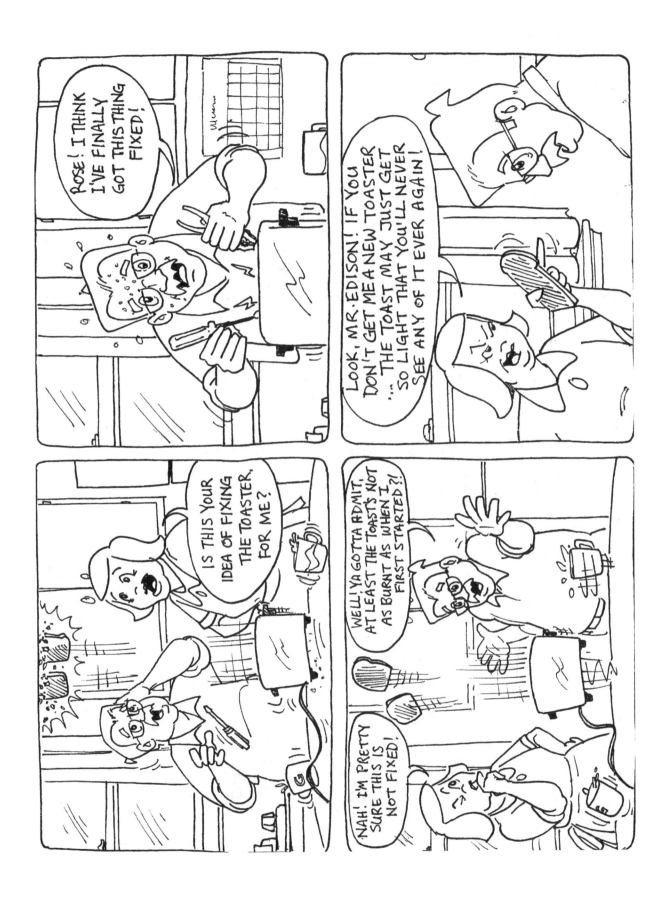

106

109

122

141

144

155

157

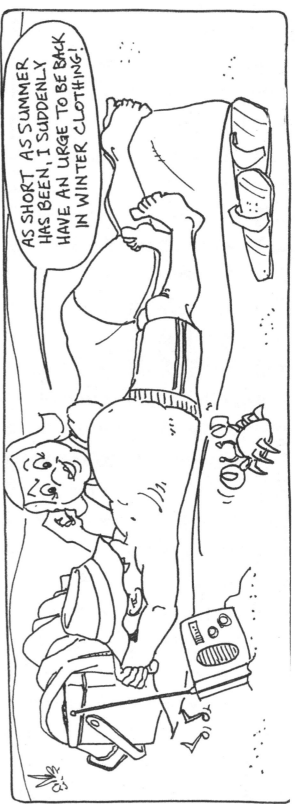

164

173

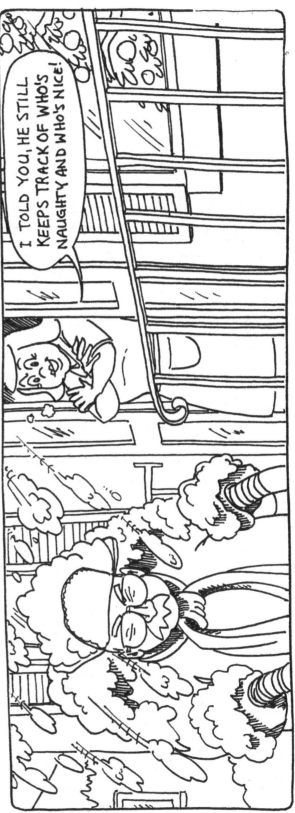

189

194

**Breaks Over**                    Back to work

_____
_____
_____
_____
_____
_____
_____
_____
_____
_____
_____
_____
_____
_____
_____
_____

Time Outs                    Together Times

_____
_____
_____
_____
_____
_____
_____
_____
_____
_____
_____
_____
_____
_____

When you've got a minute